God's true king

David

by Nathan Buttery

God's true king

a good book guide on king david

© Nathan Buttery/The Good Book Company, 2006. Reprinted 2009, 2011.

Series Consultants: Tim Chester, Tim Thornborough,

Anne Woodcock, Carl Laferton

The Good Book Company

Tel (UK): 0345-225-0880

Tel (int): + (44) 208-942-0880

Tel: (US): 866 244 2165

Email: admin@thegoodbook.co.uk

Websites

UK: www.thegoodbook.co.uk

N America: www.thegoodbook.com

Australia: www.thegoodbook.com.au

New Zealand: www.thegoodbook.co.nz

Unless indicated, all Scripture references are taken from the HOLY BIBLE, NEW
INTERNATIONAL VERSION. Copyright © 1973, 1978, 1984 International Bible Society.
Used by permission.

ISBN: 9781904889984

Printed in China

CONTENTS

Introduction   4

Why study God's true king?   5

1. An unexpected choice   7
   1 Samuel 16

2. An impossible victory   12
   1 Samuel 17

3. An amazing promise   17
   2 Samuel 7

4. An abject sinner   21
   2 Samuel 11 – 12

5. An undeserved forgiveness   26
   Psalm 51

6. An awesome God   30
   2 Samuel 22

   Leader's Guide   37

introduction: good book guides

Every Bible-study group is different—yours may take place in a church building, in a home or in a cafe, on a train, over a leisurely mid-morning coffee or squashed into a 30-minute lunch break. Your group may include new Christians, mature Christians, non-Christians, mums and tots, students, businessmen or teens. That's why we've designed these *Good Book Guides* to be flexible for use in many different situations.

Our aim in each session is to uncover the meaning of a passage, and see how it fits into the "big picture" of the Bible. But that can never be the end. We also need to appropriately apply what we have discovered to our lives. Let's take a look at what is included:

⊕ **Talkabout:** Most groups need to "break the ice" at the beginning of a session, and here's the question that will do that. It's designed to get people talking around a subject that will be covered in the course of the Bible study.

⊥ **Investigate:** The Bible text for each session is broken up into manageable chunks, with questions that aim to help you understand what the passage is about. **The Leader's Guide** contains **guidance on questions**, and sometimes ⊗ additional "follow-up" questions.

⊡ **Explore more (optional):** These questions will help you connect what you have learned to other parts of the Bible, so you can begin to fit it all together like a jig-saw; or occasionally look at a part of the passage that's not dealt with in detail in the main study.

⊖ **Apply:** As you go through a Bible study, you'll keep coming across **apply** sections. These are questions to get the group discussing what the Bible teaching means in practice for you and your church. ⊡ **Getting personal** is an opportunity for you to think, plan and pray about the changes that you personally may need to make as a result of what you have learned.

⬆ **Pray:** We want to encourage prayer that is rooted in God's word—in line with His concerns, purposes and promises. So each session ends with an opportunity to review the truths and challenges highlighted by the Bible study, and turn them into prayers of request and thanksgiving.

The **Leader's Guide** and introduction provide historical background information, explanations of the Bible texts for each session, and guidance on how best to help people uncover the truths of God's word.

why study God's true king?

The story of his battle with Goliath is the stuff of legends: an unknown, unlikely-looking youth defiantly takes on the ultimate enemy weapon— an enormous and unconquered super-warrior. He sets out unprotected and alone, yet astonishingly, he slaughters the evil giant—the enemy is routed and David wins total victory for his people.

David stands out in the Old Testament history of God's people, Israel. He is a magnetic and inspiring figure.

But then the stories and psalms reveal other "Davids"—the desperate outlaw and the broken sinner, as well as the magnificent king and "lover" of God. It's easy to see why the story of David and Goliath is still so popular. We love David the hero, the shepherd boy who became king of Israel, chosen by God as a man "after his own heart". But what about David the despised "worm", the hot-tempered bully, the weak father, the lustful playboy and the coldly calculating murderer? Did God really know what He was doing when He chose David?!

God doesn't speak to us in dry, abstract propositions—He loves to use vivid pictures, and David is a fantastic illustrated lesson for us. We warm to his character, his bold defiance of God's enemies, his humility and tender heart—humans have always wanted someone like this to look up to and be inspired by. But then he lets everyone down big time; his life becomes mired in selfish greed, callous cruelty and brazen lies. Even this "man after [God's] own heart" cannot help us because he cannot help himself.

We need a greater hero.

So the story of David isn't just a lesson in the "secrets" of David's success or the reasons for his many failures. It uncovers the bigger story of that greater hero—Jesus—giving us glimpses of His complete victory over our greatest enemies, sin and death itself. Jesus' true kingship will never fail and His perfect salvation is what we all need.

In just six sessions, you will learn how this weak king, David, points to the ultimate king, Jesus—despised like the "worm" of David's psalm and killed, yet finally winning total victory for His people over sin and death.

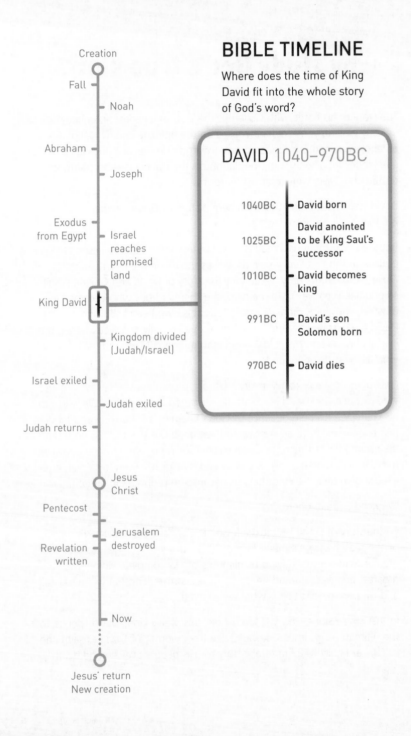

BIBLE TIMELINE

Where does the time of King David fit into the whole story of God's word?

Creation
Fall
Noah
Abraham
Joseph
Exodus from Egypt
Israel reaches promised land
King David
Kingdom divided (Judah/Israel)
Israel exiled
Judah exiled
Judah returns
Jesus Christ
Pentecost
Jerusalem destroyed
Revelation written
Now
Jesus' return
New creation

DAVID 1040–970BC

1040BC	David born
1025BC	David anointed to be King Saul's successor
1010BC	David becomes king
991BC	David's son Solomon born
970BC	David dies

1 Samuel 16
AN UNEXPECTED CHOICE

⊕ talkabout

1. Think about the way in which most people picture "success". As a group, come up with a popular description of a "successful" person. By contrast, how do you think Christians would describe a successful person?

When God chose Samuel to be His prophet to the people of Israel, things were bad. There was a crisis of leadership in Israel, and no one to lead. Yet the books of Samuel teach us that God is the King and He rules His people. He will not leave them to fall into spiritual decay. 1 and 2 Samuel tell the story of Israel's progress from chaos to order—from a land without any leadership to a land ruled by their greatest king, David.

But not only will we learn about God's dealings with David and how David responded, we will also see how David received some amazing promises, which only found their fulfilment in "great David's greater Son"—Jesus Christ. Despite his greatness, ultimately David was just a weak and sinful human; but he points us forward to the great King Jesus and helps us to see how God is our true King, controlling history and saving His people.

In this chapter, God chooses the king "after his own heart".

⊕ investigate

▶ **Read 1 Samuel 16 v 1-13:**
God's choice of David

2. Why had God rejected Saul (v 1)? See 1 Samuel 13 v 7b-14 and 15 v 24-26.

> **DICTIONARY**
>
> **Saul (v 1):** the current king of Israel.
> **Heifer (v 2):** cow.
> **Anoint (v 3):** pour oil over, as a sign of being specially chosen by God for a particular task.

3. Why was Samuel worried (v 2)? See also 1 Samuel 10 v 1.

4. Was there a need to be worried, do you think? Why/why not?

5. What do God's words (1 Samuel 16 v 1-3) show us about His plans (13 v 14)?

6. What did Samuel do in response to God's words?

➔ apply

7. In what situations will this truth—that God is in total control of His plans—be a comfort to us as Christians?

• What can Samuel's actions in v 4 teach us about trust and obedience?

• What will it mean for us to trust and obey God in the situations we have just discussed?

⊞ **investigate**

8. On what grounds did Samuel choose Eliab?

9. What did God say was wrong with Samuel's way of choosing the king?

10. **Read 1 Samuel 13 v 14.** Why did God choose David?

⊡ **explore more**

▶ **Read 1 Corinthians 1 v 20-31**

What can we learn from these verses about the way in which God acts and the people He chooses?

How can we see this in:
- *Jesus?*
- *the Christian message (the gospel)?*
- *Christians and the church?*

⊟ apply

11. In what ways do we make the same error as Samuel; for example, in our attitudes to others or to the gospel?

- Why are Jesus and the message of the cross often rejected by people? Should this worry us? Why/why not?

⊡ getting personal

In what ways are you tempted to be ashamed of the gospel because of its apparent "weakness"? Plan and pray about ways you need to change.

⊡ investigate

▶ Read 1 Samuel 16 v 14-23: God's placing of David

12. How did David conduct himself during this time?

13. What does the tragic picture of Saul here teach us about God's character?

⮕ apply

14. How does Saul stand as a warning for us today?

⬆ pray

Thank God that He uses the foolish things of this world to shame the wise. Thank Him that through the "folly" of the cross and the "weakness" of Christ He saves men and women like us!

Confess those times where you have not trusted that God is in total control of His plans, or where you have judged others by outward appearances rather than by looking at the heart.

Ask God to help you be like David—someone after His own heart—and not like Saul!

2 1 Samuel 17
AN IMPOSSIBLE VICTORY

The story so far

God chose the shepherd-boy, David, to be king of Israel, because while man looks at the outward appearance, the LORD looks at the heart.

⊕ talkabout

1. Share some frequently-heard views about what could be the greatest "enemy" that faces the human race today, and how this enemy can be defeated. Discuss how the Bible answers these questions differently.

⊕ investigate

We learned from the previous session that David is God's chosen king. He is the unlikely choice and yet, God is the one who looks not on outward appearances, but at the heart. In this chapter God shows His choice to be right by defeating the enemies of Israel through His anointed king and upholding His name, even though David is just a young man. David succeeds where Israel fails and, while everyone else writes him off, assessing him by outward appearances, yet with the Lord he is victorious. In doing this David points forward to another from his family line who will defeat God's enemies fully and finally on a cross, and will uphold God's name and His glory.

▶ Read 1 Samuel 17

It's a long passage but a great read!

DICTIONARY

Exempt (v 25): make free from.
Uncircumcised (v 26): a way of saying "not part of God's people".

2. Having read through this familiar passage, what do you think is the main point of the story?

3. What is the heart of the problem that Israel faces in Goliath (v 8-11)?

4. How does the writer show the "weakness" of David (v 12-19)?

5. How is David despised and rejected throughout the story?
Think about his conversations with:
• Eliab (v 28-29)   • Saul (v 32-39)   • Goliath (v 42-44)
How do each of these three look on "the outward appearance" of David?
And how does David respond in each of the situations?

⊡ **explore more**

optional

▶ **Read Colossians 2 v 13-15**

Find the parallels between:
- *Israel's predicament and that of sinful people everywhere.*
- *David's experiences and actions in 1 Samuel 17 and those of Jesus.*
- *the outcome of David's battle with Goliath and the outcome of Christ's death on the cross.*

➔ apply

6. In what ways do people today fall into the error of Eliab, Saul and Goliath, by regarding God's true King, Jesus, as weak and irrelevant?

• How can Christians contribute to this wrong view of Jesus?

⋯ getting personal

What could your actions and words be saying about Jesus Christ to others?
In what ways do you need to change, so that those around you will understand more truly what God's true King is like?

⬇ investigate

7. What is David's chief concern throughout the story (v 26, 36, 45)?

8. Why is it that David succeeds? (See also 1 Samuel 2 v 9b-10.) Why is he so confident (v 46-47)?

9. How do the Israelites respond to David's victory (v 52-53)?

⊡ explore more

In 1 Samuel 17 the Israelites benefited from the anointed king's victory over the enemy of God.

▸ **Read Ephesians 1 v 3-11**

What benefits do we receive through the victory of God's anointed King, Jesus?

⊝ apply

10. **Read Ephesians 6 v 12.** What "Goliath" is the church called upon to fight?

- What can we learn from this story about how this "Goliath" will be overcome? Think about:
  - God's provision for Israel's need.
  - the way David acts in this situation.
  - the Israelites' response to David's victory.

See also 1 John 5 v 4b-5.

- How will confidence that Christ's church is on the winning side, despite our weak appearance, affect the way we live as Christians?

11. What would you now say is the main point of 1 Samuel 17?

⬆ **pray**

What has God's true King, Jesus, done for you? Spend time thanking God for these things.

Pray for people you know who regard Jesus Christ as weak and irrelevant, and not worthy of their trust.

Look again at the areas of your life mentioned in the last *getting personal* and ask God to help you change.

3 2 Samuel 7
AN AMAZING PROMISE

The story so far

God chose the shepherd-boy, David, to be king of Israel, because while man looks at the outward appearance, the LORD looks at the heart.

David, anointed by God but rejected by men, won a seemingly impossible victory over God's people's enemies—a picture of King Jesus' victory.

⊕ talkabout

1. What sorts of promises do we commonly make? How good are we at keeping them? What promises can you think of that God has made? What evidence is there for the claim that God's promises never fail?

⊕ investigate

So far, we have seen how God has raised up His chosen king, David, to the throne of Israel. And through him, God has brought about victory over Israel's enemies. But in 2 Samuel 7 we discover that there is much more to come. Through David's family line, an even greater blessing will come to God's people. Sadly, the history of Israel in 1 and 2 Kings shows that no one in the Old Testament fulfils the high standards of this promise. Only one will fulfil the prophecy given to David in 2 Samuel 7; this is the one to whom the whole Old Testament looks forward—Jesus, "great David's greater Son".

In 2 Samuel 7 we will look at God's promises and then David's response.

> ▶ Read 2 Samuel 7 v 1-17: God's promises

DICTIONARY

Cedar (v 2, 7): a type of wood.
Offspring (v 12): children.
Endure (v 16): go on.

2. Describe the political and military situation that David faces at the beginning of 2 Samuel 7.

3. What is the unspoken meaning behind David's statement in verse 2?

4. How do the following verses prove Nathan's reply in verse 3 wrong? What does this teach us about human leaders?

5. What do we learn about God's character in verses 5-7? What should we remember when we are keen to "do something for God"?

6. What does God promise to David personally (v 8-9, 11b)?

7. What does God promise about David's descendant (v 12-16)?

8. What does God promise to His people (v 10)?

📖 **explore more**

optional
Look again at the promises made to David, particularly those about his descendant and God's people. How would they be fulfilled?

David's descendant
What is the temple that would be built? (See 1 Kings 8 v 17-19 and John 2 v 19-21.)
Who would be the son (v 14) whose kingdom would last forever (v 13)? (See Mark 1 v 11 and Revelation 5 v 13.)
How and why would the son be punished (v 14)? (See 2 Corinthians 5 v 21 and Galatians 3 v 13.)
How and why would God's everlasting love (v 15) be shown to the son? (See John 10 v 17 and Romans 1 v 4.)

God's people
How would v 10-11a be fulfilled? (See Revelation 21 v 1-4 and 22-27.)

➡ **apply**

9. Today Christians look forward to the promised return of Jesus Christ in power and glory. What confidence in God do the fulfilled promises of 2 Samuel 7 give us?
- What new things can we see about Jesus and His work for us, as we learn about God's promises to David and the history of their fulfilment?
- How should confidence in Christ's return affect the way we live now?

😊 **getting personal**

How much do you look forward to Christ's return? Or do you wonder if it will ever happen? How can you be helped, and help others, to have confidence in the promises of God not yet fulfilled?

⬇ investigate

❯ Read 2 Samuel 7 v 18-29: David's response

10. What does David praise God for (v 18-24)?

11. What does David pray for (v 25-29)?

➔ apply

12. Is our praise and adoration marked by similar things? If not, why not? If we prayed like David, what would have to change about the content of our prayers?

⊡ getting personal

Think of one change that you need to make in the way you pray, as a result of what you have learned in this session. Plan to make that change in the next week.

⬆ pray

Thank God for the fulfilment of His promises to David in Jesus. Why not spend time praying through them, as David did?

Pray for people you know who do not trust God.

Ask God to help you have confidence as you wait for the promised return of Jesus Christ, and to live in the light of that glorious and certain event.

4 2 Samuel 11 – 12
AN ABJECT SINNER

The story so far

God chose the shepherd-boy, David, to be king of Israel, because while man looks at the outward appearance, the LORD looks at the heart.

David, anointed by God but rejected by men, won a seemingly impossible victory over God's people's enemies—a picture of King Jesus' victory.

God promised David one of his descendants would rule for ever, as God's Son, and that His people would enjoy a perfect land—promises which come true in the life, death, resurrection and return of David's descendant, Jesus.

⊕ talkabout

1. Have you ever been "knocked off balance" by the sinfulness of a fellow-Christian? Do you ever surprise yourself by how sinful you can be? Without letting out confidential information or mentioning details that can reveal identities, discuss why you were so unprepared for what happened.

⊕ investigate: David's sin

Up to this point, David seems very impressive. He has had wonderful promises from God, he has brought the ark to Jerusalem, and, by the end of 2 Samuel 10, many of David's enemies have been conquered.

But this chapter shows how flawed David really was. It is a mistake to think that David was near perfect and that this episode is out of character. Certainly, he loved the Lord and was godly. And yet here we see the man as he really was—a weak sinner.

These chapters should not surprise us. They stand as lessons first, in the dire consequences of sin, and second, in the wonderful grace of God. It is all the more remarkable that God uses weak sinful humans to further His amazing plans and promises!

▶ Read 2 Samuel 11 v 1-27

2. What is the train of events that led to David's sin? At what points could he have stopped?

DICTIONARY

Ark (v 11): a rectangular box, covered in gold, with two angels on the lid. The space between the angels was where God's presence particularly dwelled. David had brought it into Jerusalem (2 Samuel 6), but it sometimes went with Israel's army when they were fighting.

⤷ apply

3. What do these verses teach us about temptation? Can we learn anything about resisting temptation?

⊡ getting personal

Think of one area of your life in which you are struggling to resist temptation at present. In what situations do you give in to that temptation? What can you do to avoid those situations or help yourself resist that temptation?

⬇ investigate: the consequences

4. How did David try and cover up his sin?

5. How does David's behaviour compare to that of Uriah in this chapter?

6. By the end of the chapter all looks well. But what does the writer remind us of in verse 27? Why is this so significant?

▶ Read 2 Samuel 12 v 1-13a

7. How does Nathan's story get David to see his sin?
What does this reveal about sinful human hearts?

8. What does Nathan say the real problem is?

9. What is God's judgment on David's sin?

10. How does God show grace towards David in this passage?

11. What is David's reaction to God's word? (Compare David's response in verse 13 with that of Saul in 1 Samuel 13 v 11-15 and 15 v 19-26.)

⊟ apply

12. What do these verses teach us about God's judgment? What do they teach us about the importance of listening to the "word of the LORD"?

⊡ getting personal

In what areas are you tempted to "despise the word of the LORD"?

⊡ investigate: God's forgiveness

▶ **Read 2 Samuel 12 v 13-25**

13. How can God forgive this sin? What should happen to David, according to Leviticus 20 v 10 and 24 v 17? Compare Romans 3 v 23-26.

14. What do the loss of David's illegitimate child, and the birth of Solomon, tell us about how God deals with sin?

⊖ **apply**

15. Looking back over the whole story, what have you learned about...
• human hearts and sin's consequences?

• God's judgment?

• God's forgiveness?

⬆ **pray**

Think about what you have learned...
• What can you praise God for?

• What do you need to ask His forgiveness for?

• What do you need to ask His help for?

5 Psalm 51
AN UNDESERVED FORGIVENESS

The story so far

David—anointed by God as Israel's king, but rejected by men—won a seemingly impossible victory over God's people's enemies—a picture of King Jesus' victory.

God promised David one of his descendants would rule for ever, as God's Son, and that His people would enjoy a perfect land—promises which come true in the life, death, resurrection and return of David's descendant, Jesus.

King David committed adultery and murder, which God saw and judged. But sin can also be forgiven by God.

⊕ talkabout

1. How often do we hear the word "forgiveness" in our society? What words are more likely to be used when someone has been wronged?

⊕ investigate

As the heading to this psalm suggests, it was written in the aftermath of 2 Samuel 11–12. Last session we saw how David was plunged into the depths of sin as an adulterer, liar, murderer and cheat. But the word of God came to him in the form of Nathan the prophet and so his restoration began. If the story in 2 Samuel 11–12 tells us the details of the sin, then this psalm teaches us what was going on in David's heart. And yet, it also speaks to each one of us who wrestles with sin, and shows us the wonderful depths of God's love in forgiving the sinner. We also learn what is involved for our part—heart-felt repentance.

> **Read Psalm 51 v 1-5: Confession**

2. On what grounds does David appeal to God for forgiveness (v 1-2)?

3. What has David discovered about himself (v 3-5)?

4. How do you think he has come to this discovery (see 2 Samuel 12, especially verses 9a and 11a)?

→ apply

5. Why is it important that we understand God's character as revealed in His word?
  • How will this help us in the Christian life?
  • What happens when we have a poor understanding of our own sin?

⊡ getting personal

Do you see yourself as David saw himself? If not, why not? What can you do to gain a better understanding of God's character and your sin?

⊙ investigate

❯ Read Psalm 51 v 6-8: Confidence

6. How is David's confidence seen in these verses?

⊡ explore more

optional

Do you think the Christian's confidence should be greater or lesser than David's? Why do you think that? See Colossians 1 v 25-26.

Our Bible translations mask the fact that the verbs in Ps 51 v 6b-8 are future tense—"you will teach me"… "you will cleanse me". David was looking forward to these things. But the New Testament uses present or past tenses to speak about the same experience for Christians.

How have Christians been taught "wisdom in the inmost place" by God? See 1 John 2 v 20-27 (especially v 20 and 27). What is that wisdom? See Colossians 2 v 3 and 2 Timothy 3 v 15.
How have Christians been "cleansed" and "washed" by God? See John 15 v 3, Ephesians 5 v 25-26 and Titus 3 v 4-5.
So what do people need to become acceptable (clean) to God and to be truly wise? What does this mean for Christian outreach and evangelism?

❯ Read Psalm 51 v 9-13: Renewal

7. What are the various longings that David expresses in these verses?
- v 9
- v 10
- v 11
- v 12

8. Looking at verse 13, what is David's aim now he has been forgiven?

▶ Read Psalm 51 v 14-19: Response

9. What other longings and intentions make up David's response to God in these verses?

- v 14-15

- v 16-17

- v 18-19

10. What is it that God requires of us in verses 16-17?

⊡ apply

11. How will we act, as individual Christians and as churches, if we share these longings that David has spoken about in Psalm 51?
- How does David's attitude in verse 13 challenge us?

⊡ getting personal

How much do you share David's longings and responses to God? Are there any that are missing from your life? What will you do about that?

⊡ pray

What have you learned from this psalm about God's dealings with us? Give Him praise and thanks for those things.

Pray for those you know who don't understand God's character and their own sinfulness, and so have no understanding of God's amazing grace.

Ask God to help you remember the encouragements and act on the challenges of this psalm.

6 2 Samuel 22
AN AWESOME GOD

> ## The story so far
>
> God promised David one of his descendants would rule for ever, as God's Son, and that His people would enjoy a perfect land—promises which come true in the life, death, resurrection and return of David's descendant, Jesus.
>
> King David committed adultery and murder, which God saw and judged. But God's people can confess their sins and know that they are forgiven by Him, just as David did.

⊕ talkabout

1. Share some commonly-held views about what God is like. Where do these views come from? If you, as a Christian, had the opportunity to talk to someone with one of these views about what God is like, what points would you try to get across?

⊕ investigate: David's God

This final session brings us to the end of the books of 1 and 2 Samuel, but to the heart of David. In 2 Samuel 22 David is looking back over certain events in his life (see v 1), and remembering how God has watched over him. David shows his deep understanding of the God he serves, and, with the benefit of hindsight, he can now see that God's hand has been at work, which causes him to praise.

But more than that, David's hindsight of the past helps him to live with foresight in the present. David's only concern is to glorify God, who has kept him and rescued him on countless occasions. As Christians, we can appreciate much of what David says as we also know it to be true through Jesus. The challenge to us is whether the God we claim to know is the same as David's, or whether our view of God is rather shallow in comparison. David truly knew God!

▶ Read 2 Samuel 22 v 1-20

2. In verses 2-4, how many different images does David use to describe God? How does each image help us to understand God better?

3. What was David's first port of call in his time of distress?

4. What do verses 8-20 show us about David's understanding of God? Are there any hints from these verses as to where David's understanding of God came from? (Compare Exodus 19 v 18.)

5. In verses 17-20, David records three ways in which God has saved him. What are they?

⊡ apply

6. What things can prevent us from praying as David did (v 7) when we are in difficulty?

- How will praying help us in these situations?

- How would an understanding of God, like David's, help us to live as Christians?

- How can we help ourselves to develop this kind of understanding and experience of God?

⊡ getting personal

What has been your first reaction in times of trouble? Like David's, in verse 7? If not, why not? How big is your God?

⊥ investigate: David's righteousness

> **❯ Read 2 Samuel 22 v 21-31**

7. What do these verses tell us about David's desires and heart?

⊡ explore more

optional

What is David not saying in these verses? (Compare Psalm 51. See also Romans 3 v 10-12.)

So what is he saying? (See Proverbs 3 v 5-6 and Matthew 5 v 1-12).

*How have verses 21-25 been fulfilled literally? (See 1 Peter 2 v 22.)
How can these verses be true of Christians? (See 2 Corinthians 5 v 21.)*

⊥ investigate: David's hope

> **❯ Read 2 Samuel 22 v 31-51**

8. How is David able to win victory over his enemies?

9. How are David's victories over his enemies described? What impression does this give?

⊡ **explore more**

How are these verses fulfilled in Jesus? Think about:

- *His victory (v 32-43): see Hebrews 2 v 14-15; Colossians 2 v 13-15.*

- *His rule over the nations (v 44-46): see Matthew 25 v 31-46; Revelation 19 v 11-16.*

- *His final exaltation (v 47-52): see Philippians 2 v 9-11.*

→ **apply**

10. What qualities have you seen in the life of David, which, as a Christian, you would like to imitate in your own life?

- From looking at the life of God's king, David, what have you learned about God's true King, Jesus? And how will that affect your life?

⊡ **getting personal**

Can you see, as David did, how God has worked in the past—both in history and in your own experience? Do you have confidence, like David, of God's wonderful future for you?

How could grateful hindsight and confident foresight affect the way you live now?

⬆ pray

Praise God for what He has done in the past, for how He has made you righteous, and for what He is going to do in the future.

Ask God to help you put into practice particular lessons that you have learned from the life of David.

Take some words from 2 Samuel 22 which have particularly struck you; turn them into your own heartfelt prayer to God.

God's true king

David

LEADER'S GUIDE

Leader's Guide

INTRODUCTION

Leading a Bible study can be a bit like herding cats—everyone has a different idea of what the passage could be about, and a different line of enquiry that they want to pursue. But a good group leader is more than someone who just referees this kind of discussion. You will want to:

• correctly understand and handle the Bible passage. But also…

• encourage and train the people in your group to do this for themselves. Don't fall into the trap of spoon-feeding people by simply passing on the information in the Leader's Guide. Then…

• make sure that no Bible study is finished without everyone knowing how the passage is relevant for them. What changes do you all need to make in the light of the things you have been learning? And finally…

• encourage the group to turn all that has been learned and discussed into prayer.

Your Bible-study group is unique, and you are likely to know better than anyone the capabilities, backgrounds and circumstances of the people you are leading. That's why we've designed these guides with a number of optional features. If they're a quiet bunch, you might want to spend longer on talkabout. If your time is limited, you can choose to skip explore more, or get people to look at these questions at home. Can't get enough of Bible study? Well, some studies have optional extra homework projects. As leader, you can adapt and select the material to the needs of your particular group.

So what's in the Leader's Guide? The main thing that this Leader's Guide will help you to do is to understand the major teaching points in the passage you are studying, and how to apply them. As well as guidance on the questions, the Leader's Guide for each session contains the following important sections:

THE BIG IDEA

One key sentence will give you the main point of the session. This is what you should be aiming to have fixed in people's minds as they leave the Bible study. And it's the point you need to head back towards when the discussion goes off at a tangent.

SUMMARY

An overview of the passage, including plenty of useful historical background information.

So let's take a look at the various different features of a Good Book Guide:

⊕ talkabout

Each session kicks off with a discussion question, based on the group's opinions or experiences. It's designed to get people talking and thinking in a general way about the main subject of the Bible study.

⊥ investigate

The first thing you and your group need to know is what the Bible passage is about, which is the purpose of these questions. But watch out—people may come up with answers based on their experiences or teaching they have heard in the past, without referring to the passage at all. It's amazing how often we can get through a Bible study without actually looking at the Bible! If you're stuck for an answer, the Leader's Guide contains guidance on questions. These are the answers to direct your group to. This information isn't meant to be read out to people—ideally, you want them to discover these answers from the Bible for themselves. Sometimes there are optional follow-up questions (see ⊻ in guidance on questions) to help you help your group get to the answer.

⊡ explore more

These questions generally point people to other relevant parts of the Bible. They are useful for helping your group to see how the passage fits into the "big picture" of the whole Bible. These sections are OPTIONAL—only use them if you have time. Remember that it's better to finish in good time having really grasped one big thing from the passage, than to try and cram everything in.

⊟ apply

We want to encourage you to spend more time working at application—too often, it is simply tacked on at the end. In the Good Book Guides, apply sections are mixed in with the investigate sections of the study. We hope that people will realise that application is not just an optional extra, but rather, the whole purpose of studying the Bible. We do Bible study so that our lives can be changed by what we hear from God's word. If you skip the application, the Bible study hasn't achieved its purpose.

These questions draw out practical lessons that we can all learn from the Bible passage. You can review what has been learned so far, and think about practical differences that this should make in our churches and our lives. The group gets the opportunity to talk about what they personally have learned.

⊡ getting personal

These can be done at home, but it is well worth allowing a few moments of quiet reflection during the study for each person to think and pray about specific changes they need to make in their own lives. Why not have a time for reporting back at the beginning of the following session, so that everyone can be encouraged and challenged by one another to make application a priority?

⬆ pray

In Acts 4 v 25-30 the first Christians quoted Psalm 2 as they prayed in response to the persecution of the apostles by the Jewish religious leaders. Today however, it's not as common for Christians to base prayers on the truths of God's word as it once was. As a result, our prayers tend to be weak, superficial and self-centred rather than bold, visionary and God-centred.

The prayer section is based on what has been learned from the Bible passage. How different our prayer times would be if we were genuinely responding to what God has said to us through His word.

1 and 2 Samuel: an introduction

This introduction should help you as a group leader to understand clearly the important themes and issues that are covered in each session as you look through the main events of David's life and reign.

HISTORICAL BACKGROUND

Judges: 1 & 2 Samuel (they are a complete unit) describe a transition period in Israel's history. The earlier book of Judges covers the period before 1 & 2 Samuel. Israel, under the leadership of Joshua, had taken the land promised to them by God, but then fell into spiritual decline. The Israelites ignored God and thus were constantly menaced by enemies which they had failed to conquer. God repeatedly raised up "judges" or rescuers to save the people.

The last judges: This is the situation at the beginning of 1 Samuel. Eli is the "judge" in charge (see 1 Sam 4 v 18 NIV footnote), and his sons, Hophni and Phinehas, are the priests—but it is clear that they are corrupt. Yet while this old leadership is dying off, God is quietly raising up a new leader—Samuel. The prayer of Hannah, Samuel's mother (1 Sam 2 v 1-10), sets out many of the key themes of the books (compare 1 Sam 2 v 9b-10 and 2 Sam 22 v 51).

Transition: Samuel is the man God has chosen to lead Israel into the next period of their history, from judges to kings. Samuel is the last of the judges (1 Sam 7 v 15); but he is also the first of those prophets who will keep the kings in check (3 v 20). Samuel is not the first prophet, but from this point onwards, prophets have a special job to speak God's word not only to the nation, but also to the king. For the rest of Israel's history in the Old Testament, God will raise up a king, but also a prophet to keep him in check. Both will be appointed by God, though the relationship will often be stormy!

The new kingdom: 1 & 2 Samuel are basically a description of how the kingship came into being, and particularly, how David's kingship was exercised. But supremely, they teach us about God, the King of Israel and the One behind the earthly kings. Israel asks for a king in 1 Sam 8, and though their motives are wrong (see v 19-20), God grants their request. This shows that, in God's mind, kingship in itself is not necessarily wrong; the key point is that the king must be a godly man (see Deuteronomy 17 v 14-20). Saul is the first choice, but he makes the mistake of trying to do Samuel's job and from then on, his fate is sealed (see 1 Sam 13 v 7b-14; 15 v 24-26, 34-35). That leads to David, God's choice of king (13 v 14).

David's reign: David is Israel's most impressive king. Under him, Israel is fully established and Jerusalem becomes the capital, where the ark of the covenant is based. In 2 Sam 7 v 1 David has "rest"—he has defeated all the enemy countries surrounding Israel. This is significant!

The ultimate King: The real theme of the account of David is not David at all, but the God he served. Most importantly, through God's anointed one or "messiah", David, we get a preview (though often a pale, shadowy one) of God's ultimate Messiah. God's promises to David in 2 Sam 7 show that his kingdom will never end. It is through David's line that we will see Jesus, great David's greater Son. So we will learn, not just about David and how God deals with this remarkable individual, but through David we will learn about Jesus Christ.

1

1 Samuel 16
AN UNEXPECTED CHOICE

THE BIG IDEA
Man looks at the outward appearance but the Lord looks at the heart.

SUMMARY
Here we meet David for the first time and see the one who is described as a man after God's own heart (1 Samuel 13 v 14). The key to chapter 16 comes in verse 7. How we "see" things is a key theme throughout the books of Samuel, and here we discover that God "sees" not according to man's ways; for "the Lord looks at the heart". The man God chooses is not the one we would have picked, yet he is the right man for the job. Nor would we have picked the man Jesus, or His death on the cross as the way to save the world. Yet that is always God's way—He is full of surprises!

In order to introduce the study, it's worthwhile taking a few minutes to set the historical scene. You could reproduce the timeline (p 6) on a larger scale, to show your group how Israel had developed by the time of Samuel, and then extend it to include more details from the early chapters of 1 Samuel, so that people can see where we are up to in the story. Perhaps include the death of Eli and his sons, the rise of Samuel and the fall of Saul. You may want to read some of the verses connected with Saul's downfall as well (see Q2 below), but don't get carried away! We won't need much detail, just enough to set the context.

GUIDANCE ON QUESTIONS
1. Think about the way in which most people picture "success". As a group, come up with a popular description of a "successful" person. By contrast, how do you think Christians would describe a successful person? You might like to point out that God's criteria are often counter cultural! True "success" must be determined by Him!

2. Why had God rejected Saul (v 1)? See 1 Samuel 13 v 7b-14 and 15 v 24-26. In 1 Sam 13, Saul had clearly disobeyed God's command (see v 13) by taking on himself the responsibility of making an offering to God, instead of waiting for Samuel, Israel's judge and prophet and therefore God's appointed representative.

Clearly, it was crucially important to God that the right person made an offering at the right place and in the right way (see also Joshua 22 v 10-18). In 1 Samuel 15, Saul had still not learned his lesson; instead of obeying God's clear command (v 3), he had followed his own idea of what he thought would please Him (v 20-21). Saul's rejection of God's word (v 26) was not a one-off mistake, but a persistent attitude of rebellion.

3. Why was Samuel worried (v 2)? See also 1 Samuel 10 v 1. Samuel was afraid that Saul would kill him (v 2). Also, Samuel had anointed Saul (10 v 1) and had got the kingship off to a start. He may have felt some responsibility, now that, humanly speaking, things looked very shaky.

4. Was there a need to be worried, do you think? Why/why not? Samuel's fear (v 2) can be understood from a human point of view. But he was forgetting that God is behind all these events. The true King never loses control of events in His kingdom! Samuel forgot, albeit temporarily, that God already had another king up His sleeve (see 13 v 14).

5. What do God's words (1 Samuel 16 v 1-3) show us about His plans (13 v 14)? Sooner or later God's plans are carried out.

6. What did Samuel do in response to God's words? Having heard God's final word on the matter, Samuel got on with doing "what the Lord said" (16 v 4), regardless of his grief for Saul (v 1) or his fear of what might happen (v 2). He went to Jesse's family to anoint the man that God had chosen to be the next king of Israel. Once there, Samuel ignored his own preference for Eliab, Jesse's eldest son, and instead followed what God was telling him, even though this meant that all the sons of Jesse present at the sacrifice were finally rejected. Samuel persisted in his search for the man that God had chosen until finally, David arrived and God confirmed that he was the one. In verse 13, Samuel anoints him (literally "messiahs" him). David receives the Spirit, the sign of God's equipping and enabling to lead His people. (Note that in the Old Testament, some people were given the Spirit at specific times for specific jobs eg: Exodus 31 v 3; Judges 3 v 10. Now all God's people have Him; for example, see 1 Corinthians 12 v 3.)

7. APPLY: In what situations will this truth—that God is in total control of His plans—be a comfort to us as Christians? Allow the group to come up with situations that are relevant to them. Situations in which Christians struggle to trust God and obey His revealed will may include: difficult marriages; church discipline; bringing up wayward children; illness; bereavement; the necessity of forgiveness; evangelism; persecution etc. Discuss how our experience of these kinds of situations can be transformed when we understand that God is in total control of everything.

• **What can Samuel's actions in v 4 teach us about trust and obedience?** There's an important lesson for us here, in Samuel's quiet and zealous obedience (v 4). He doesn't keep on questioning or arguing with God—he just does what is required. Things may look beyond hope for us, but God simply asks for trust that He is in control, and obedience, even if we cannot see the final outcome!

• **What will it mean for us to trust and obey God in the situations we have just discussed?** Encourage people to be practical in suggesting what they might do and pray for in the situations you have discussed.

8. On what grounds did Samuel choose Eliab? Samuel "saw" Eliab with his eyes. Eliab must have been impressive to look at because Samuel's immediate thought was that Eliab must be the Lord's anointed (v 6).

9. What did God say was wrong with Samuel's way of choosing the king? In verse 7, God told Samuel not to consider the appearance, ie: the outward features. Rather, what God considers important is the heart, which only He can see. So God's view of things is different from man's. Samuel must learn to see as God sees. In 17 v 28 we see what Eliab's heart was like. Needless to say, it is not pleasant. His outward features may have been impressive, but he was not God's man. Saul's features were also impressive (9 v 2)—commentators often note the similarities between Saul and Eliab.

If Israel had followed Samuel's instinct, then Israel could have had another Saul! Even a godly prophet gets some things wrong! But God is in control.

10. Read 1 Samuel 13 v 14. Why did God choose David? Because He alone could see that David would be a king after His own heart (13 v 14). Note that Jesse didn't even consider it worth calling David home to meet Samuel, such was his opinion of David's insignificance! No one would have thought that this shepherd boy would be God's choice, and yet he was! Verse 12 indicates that David himself had a good appearance. God is not anti appearance; rather, that is not the way in which He judges people.

EXPLORE MORE
Read 1 Corinthians 1 v 20-31. What can we learn from these verses about the way in which God acts and the people He chooses? God's ways are very different from ours. God uses people and ways of doing things that humans consider to be weak or foolish or even shameful.
How can we see this in:
• **Jesus?** In Jesus God turns the world's standards upside down! Consider how Jesus goes against the grain in terms of how the world views greatness or worth. He was despised and rejected (Isaiah 53 v 2-3). He was the King who suffered, the rejected stone that was the capstone (the most important stone in a building—1 Peter 2 v 7), the rescuer who was crucified, the Son of God who died like a criminal! If we look with the world's eyes then we miss the Saviour!
• **The Christian message (the gospel)?** The good news about Jesus seems foolish to the world because it doesn't come with miraculous signs and it doesn't

offer answers to all the questions of philosophers (1 Corinthians 1 v 22-24). It invites anyone ("dumbed down" and populist propaganda) to come into a relationship with a man who lived and died 2,000 years ago (dull and irrelevant history), and claimed to have risen from death (childish fairy stories). It offers forgiveness and eternal life to those who simply trust in Jesus as their Saviour and follow Him as their Lord (naïve and simplistic superstition)!
• **Christians and the church?** Few Christians are humanly wise, influential or of noble birth (1 Corinthians 1 v 26). All Christians are only sinners saved by grace. The church is not made up of the kind of people that we would choose if we wanted to start a movement that would change the world.

11. APPLY: In what ways do we make the same error as Samuel; for example, in our attitudes to others or to the gospel? Get people to think of situations in which they are impressed (or disappointed) by appearances. Some examples are: an evangelistic event with professional music, state-of-the-art IT resources and slick organisation may be less effective than a simple talk or discussion with a few interested non-Christians; we may be impressed by a speaker's personality, style of speaking, humour or appearance, rather than by what he says and how he says it; in church, are we more attracted to gifted, prosperous, intelligent people than to those who are quiet, unimpressive, awkward personalities or struggling with problems? What we think is impressive is often useless. What we think is useless may be very precious in God's eyes!

- **Why are Jesus and the message of the cross often rejected by people? Should this worry us? Why/why not?** People often reject the gospel of Jesus precisely because it doesn't offer them the key to happiness or success in this world, because Christians are just ordinary people, and because following Jesus means a life of sacrifice and self-denial for now. We shouldn't be worried about people rejecting the gospel of Jesus, as long it is not because of our sin. Jesus Himself was utterly rejected, even by those who had heard His teaching and witnessed His miraculous signs. Bible passages like 1 Corinthians 1 v 20-31 (see explore more above) warn us that people who are impressed by worldly wisdom or spectacular displays of power will be disappointed by God's intervention in our world. But God will win in the end. His foolishness will be seen to be wiser than human wisdom and His weakness more powerful than human strength (1 Corinthians 1 v 25).

12. How did David conduct himself during this time? What is striking in the second half of 1 Samuel, starting here, is David's godliness in the presence of Saul. Later, when Saul in his final years ruthlessly persecutes David, we see that David's godly treatment of Saul springs from his confidence that God can and will work out His purpose.

13. What does the tragic picture of Saul here teach us about God's character?

Saul is clearly deteriorating—the Spirit of the Lord leaves him (v 14). God has rejected this servant; therefore His equipping of this man is over. Saul has turned away from God and so God's judgment on Saul is to turn away from him. Instead, Saul is tormented by another spirit that is evil, which we are told is from the Lord (v 14). It is ironic that David, the one who will replace Saul as God's king, ends up in Saul's court. Saul chooses David because, unknown to him, God has already chosen David. God is working His purpose out through His anointed one and Saul, in all his disobedience and failure, can do nothing except further that purpose of God, even though it will end his own kingship. Thus, God has begun His judgment of Saul from this point, while God's anointed one is beginning to thrive. It's a sober warning of the judgment of God on those who turn away from Him!

14. APPLY: How does Saul stand as a warning for us today? Saul failed to obey God's clear command; instead he did what he thought would please God, and he did this repeatedly. The story of Saul is a stark warning that God will not tolerate disobedience for ever. Discuss with your group what clear commands of God people need to obey today and how they follow their own ideas instead—you might like to look up John 3 v 18.

Note: It may be helpful to encourage people to read next session's Bible passage, which is fairly long, beforehand.

2   2 Samuel 17
AN IMPOSSIBLE VICTORY

THE BIG IDEA

God's anointed one, rejected by men but upheld by God, wins a seemingly impossible victory for God's people.

SUMMARY

We learned from the previous study that David is God's chosen king. He is the unlikely choice and yet God is the one who looks not on outward appearances but at the heart. In this chapter God shows His choice to be right by defeating the enemies of Israel through His anointed one. David succeeds where Israel fails and, while everyone else writes him off, examining him on the outward appearances, yet with the Lord he is victorious.

The point of this story is that David, as God's anointed, defeats God's enemies and upholds God's name. It looks forward to another "David", who will defeat all of God's enemies fully and finally on a cross and will uphold God's name and glory. Where do we fit into this picture? Well, we are like the Israelites who, although unable to fight the battle themselves, still enjoy the benefits of the anointed one's victory.

This is a long passage, and you will have to decide which parts to read aloud. The core is verses 12-51. Hopefully, people will also have read it beforehand, as suggested last session.

GUIDANCE ON QUESTIONS

1. Share some frequently-heard views about what could be the greatest "enemy" that faces the human race today, and how this enemy can be defeated. Discuss how the Bible answers these questions differently.

Ideas may include: international terrorism, global warming, population growth, family breakdown etc. Solutions rely on human might, effort and ingenuity. The Bible, on the other hand, identifies humanity's greatest enemy as sin (and death—which is God's judgment on sin). And the only solution is to be rescued by God's Messiah (eg: see Romans 3 v 20-24).

2. Having read through this familiar passage, what do you think is the main point of the story? This topic is revisited in Q11 at the end of the session. Let people share ideas about the main point of the passage and don't worry about correcting them at this stage. Hopefully, by Q11 they will have come to understand for themselves the answer given in the Summary section above.

Typically, this passage is used to justify all sorts of strange things such as the challenge to "defeat the Goliaths in your life", which can be anything from school bullies to lack of self esteem! Though the Bible might address those issues elsewhere, this is certainly not the main point of the account of David's battle with Goliath. We need to remember 1 Samuel chapter 16 as we read chapter 17 (ie: David is God's anointed one, chosen to help and lead God's people). Also remember that David is a preview of God's ultimate Messiah.

3. What is the heart of the problem that Israel faces in Goliath (v 8-11)?

Israel is already facing an attack on their land and people. The Philistines have been a constant threat for many years, and Israel, the covenant people of God, have never been able to conquer them. Who will save them? The problem before the Israelites becomes even clearer as the writer shows how awesome Goliath is. Humanly speaking he is a huge figure (literally!) and yet we should have learned from chapter 16 not to trust outward appearances! Verse 9 shows that defeat will mean slavery—going back to Egypt, not literally, but figuratively! Israel is facing a test of their trust in God and their zeal for God's name. Will they just take what Goliath is hurling at them and Yahweh? Failure will be disastrous!

4. How does the writer show the "weakness" of David (v 12-19)? He is the youngest (v 14) and was not a warrior (v 15). His father treats him like a messenger boy (v 17-19) and seems not to be too bothered about the anointing of the previous chapter. And yet, David is the Lord's anointed and therefore equipped for God's service.

5. How is David despised and rejected throughout the story? Think about his conversations with:

- **Eliab (v 28-29):** David is belittled by his brother. These verses make clear why God had not chosen Eliab as king. Eliab is jealous, angry and perhaps vulnerable! He tries to squash his brother by reminding him of the sheep! He questions David's motives ("Why have you come down here?" v 28), and he maligns his character by calling David "conceited" and "wicked". The irony is that Eliab claims to be able to see into David's heart, when in fact he cannot see how God has looked on David. Eliab judges by outward appearances. He has failed to acknowledge the Lord's anointed. David simply walks away (v 30).

- **Saul (v 32-39):** He marginalises David as a silly boy (v 33). But David teaches Saul some practical theology from the fields (v 37). David knows that God is the one who has delivered him from the bear and the lion. He will deliver David again. He is absolutely confident in the power of God.

- **Goliath (v 42-44):** Again, David is viewed from the outward appearance. He's just a youngster who must be squashed. David's response is humble faith in God's power (v 45). Goliath uses the weapons of outward strength but David comes in "the name of the Lord".

EXPLORE MORE
Read Colossians 2 v 13-15. Find the parallels between:

- **Israel's predicament and that of sinful people everywhere.** Israel seemed helpless to fight against Goliath and free themselves from the threatened slavery of the Philistines (1 Sam 17 v 11). Sinners are utterly unable to help free themselves from sin; so much so that they are described as "dead" in their sins (Colossians 2 v 13).

- **David's experiences and actions in 1 Samuel 17 and those of Jesus.** David, though weak and despised in the eyes of others, took on Goliath's challenge. Jesus was willing to be weak and despised by being nailed to a cross, to defeat sin and death (Colossians 2 v 14).

- **the outcome of David's battle with Goliath and the outcome of Christ's death on the cross.** David, with just a sling and stones, was able to defeat Goliath and win victory for Israel over the entire Philistine army. Jesus, by His death on the cross, triumphed over sin and death and the evil powers behind them, and won eternal life and forgiveness for all God's people (Colossians 2 v 15).

6. APPLY: In what ways do people today fall into the error of Eliab, Saul and Goliath, by regarding God's true King, Jesus, as weak and irrelevant? While many admire Jesus, it is common for people to view Him simply as "gentle Jesus, meek and mild", as someone who was too heavenly-minded to be of much earthly use. His death is seen as a tragic end that perhaps could have been avoided if He had been more politically shrewd. He is contrasted with people like the apostle Paul, considered to be a tougher and more assertive character, who allegedly reorganised Jesus' pure religion of love and forgiveness into a system of hard dogma that would take over the world—something that Jesus Himself apparently failed to achieve. Muslims won't accept the biblical portrayal of Jesus because they cannot believe that someone crucified as a criminal could come from God.

- **How can Christians contribute to this wrong view of Jesus?** By (for example)… never speaking about Jesus, so that He becomes almost incidental to Christianity; disregarding Jesus' total lordship of their lives, so that He becomes just a divine "sugar daddy" or a shoulder to cry on when things get tough; focusing Christian ministry on achieving financial prosperity or political campaigns, which Jesus never "succeeded" with because they were never part of His agenda; etc.

7. What is David's chief concern throughout the story (v 26, 36, 45)? David's first recorded words in the Bible show his concern for God's honour among God's people (v 26). He will not stand by while a pagan insults the armies of the living God. Verses 45-47 are in some ways the climax. When Goliath defies the armies

of God, he defies the living God Himself. But David's trust is in the living God. He is confident that Goliath will be defeated precisely because Goliath stands opposed to God.

8. Why is it that David succeeds? (See also 1 Samuel 2 v 9b -10.) Why is he so confident (v 46-47)? It is the LORD who gives David victory (v 46). He knows that God's battles are not won by human strength, but only because God gives the victory to His servant (v 47). And by the end of the story we are in no doubt that God gives the victory—at the point where God's servant appears at his weakest. Hannah's prayer comes to a fulfilment (see 1 Samuel 2 v 9b-10).

9. How do the Israelites respond to David's victory (v 52-53)? They continued the fight that had already been won by David's action, by pursuing and plundering the Philistines.

EXPLORE MORE
Read Ephesians 1 v 3-11. What benefits do we receive through the victory of God's anointed King Jesus? The Israelites enjoyed the benefits of the victory which had been won by God's anointed one, David. In the same way, the Lord's Anointed, Jesus Christ, has won the victory over the devil, sin and death through His suffering, and now Christians benefit in an incredible way—we have "every spiritual blessing", according to Ephesians 1 v 3— through the victory of God's anointed King, Jesus. Christians… are chosen to be holy and blameless (v 4); are adopted as God's sons (v 4-5); receive God's glorious grace through Jesus Christ, which is "freely given" (v 6), and even "lavished" on Christians (v 8); have redemption and the forgiveness of

sins (v 7); have been given all wisdom and understanding (v 8); know the mystery of God's will, purposed in Christ (v 9). Just like the Israelites, Christians have done nothing to earn the victory—it has been given by God through the Messiah. Like the Israelites, Christians continue the fight against the enemies of God, but the foe is already defeated!

10. APPLY: Read Ephesians 6 v 12. What "Goliath" is the church called upon to fight? Christians are called to fight against the powers of this dark world and the spiritual forces of evil in the heavenly realms.

• **What can we learn from this story about how this "Goliath" will be overcome? Think about:**
  …God's provision for Israel's need?
  …the way David acts in this situation?
  …the Israelites' response to David's victory?
  See also 1 John 5 v 4b-5. God has provided a Messiah, Jesus Christ, to win the victory for us; like David, we can have

total confidence that these powers will be defeated because they defy the sovereign God; the task of the church is to continue the fight against God's enemies that have already been defeated by Christ's death on the cross.

• **How will confidence that Christ's church is on the winning side, despite our weak appearance, affect the way we live as Christians?** Areas of our lives that can be transformed by confidence of ultimate victory include faithfulness to the word of God, evangelism, persistence in doing good, enduring persecution and forgiving our enemies etc.

11. APPLY: What would you now say is the main point of 1 Samuel 17? This question looks back to Q2. Some people may want to change their view on what the passage is all about, others to stay the same. You might like to ask your group whether anything has surprised them as they've given this familiar story an in-depth look.

3 2 Samuel 7
AN AMAZING PROMISE

THE BIG IDEA
Jesus Christ is the ultimate and perfect fulfilment of God's promises to David.

SUMMARY
So far, we have seen how God has raised up His chosen king, David, to the throne of Israel. And through him, God has brought about victory over Israel's enemies. Humanly speaking, the kingdom of Israel was at its peak during the reign of David and at the

beginning of the reign of his son, Solomon. David controlled all the land that had been promised by God to His people, and the ark of God was situated in the capital, Jerusalem. God was dwelling with His people in the land He had given them, and they were enjoying His blessing.

At the start of 2 Samuel 7, we find that God has given David rest, which does not mean sleep but peace in the land. It seems as if the promises to Abraham (see Genesis

12) have at last been fulfilled. And yet, this chapter shows that there is much more to come. Through David, there will come even greater blessing to God's people.

Sadly, the history of Israel in 1 and 2 Kings shows that no one in the Old Testament fulfils the high standards of this promise. Only one will fulfil the prophecy given in 2 Samuel 7; this is the one to whom the whole Old Testament looks forward—Jesus, "great David's greater Son".

This chapter is thus a wonderful promise about the greater "David" to come and about God's faithfulness to His people. But it also contains David's godly response to the promises of God. Time may prevent you from looking in too much detail at the second half of the chapter, but it repays more study and teaches us much about how we should pray, both personally and together.

GUIDANCE ON QUESTIONS

1. What sorts of promises do we commonly make? How good are we at keeping them? What promises can you think of that God has made? What evidence is there for the claim that God's promises never fail? While the obvious conclusion is that God, unlike us, never fails to keep His promises, this is also an opportunity to remind each other of some of the many promises of God, and to point out how reasonable it is to trust God in the light of Bible history, which records the fulfilment of His promises.

2. Describe the political and military situation that David faces at the beginning of 2 Samuel 7. David is happy. God has given David "rest" from his enemies (v 1). It looks as if everything is going well.

3. What is the unspoken meaning behind David's statement in verse 2? Despite the situation Israel is enjoying, David feels that all is not well. He is expressing a desire to see a house built for God (v 2). The ark of the covenant, which represented God's presence with His people at that time, was kept in a temporary tent, the tabernacle, as prescribed by God in Exodus. David wanted a permanent place for God. Nathan, the prophet of the Lord, gives him the go-ahead (v 3). He believes the Lord is with David on this one.

4. How do the following verses prove Nathan's reply in verse 3 wrong? What does this teach us about human leaders? In verses 4-16, God's reply shows Nathan to be wrong in encouraging David to build a house for God (v 3). In effect, God says to David: Not you and not yet! Instead, He has other business for David. A small sub theme in 1 & 2 Samuel is the mistakes that God's men make eg: Eli in 1 Samuel 2; Samuel in 1 Samuel 16; and here with Nathan. God's leadership is the one to trust. Men will always let us down at some point, and fail to discern God's will properly.

5. What do we learn about God's character in verses 5-7? What should we remember when we are keen to "do something for God"? God's actions and plans reveal His character. We can understand Him from His acts and His words—He is not unknowable. So God explains to David His actions among the people of Israel: He has been with them from the start of their existence as a nation, from the exodus out of Egypt; He has not wanted a permanent dwelling. Instead, God is found at the heart of His people—where His people are, He is there. This is God's choice—He does not need to do this, as He does not need anything. When we are keen to "do something for God" we should learn from David's misguided intentions. God does not need us—instead, as we shall see, He chooses to do things for us. We, however, need Him.

6. What does God promise to David personally (v 8-9, 11b)? First, God promises to make David's name great (v 8-9). It is not David who will do something for God; God will do something for David! God is the one who brought him from obscurity and He will continue His work. Second, God will destroy David's enemies and give him "rest" (v 9a, 11b). Third, God promises to David an everlasting house or dynasty—the word in Hebrew means both (v 11c). It is not David who will build God a house, but God who will build David one. This is the most important promise, for out of this house or dynasty will come the promised Messiah. David will not see all of this fulfilled himself, but God's faithfulness to him has already been seen in his life. **Note:** God interweaves His promises for David personally, his descendant, and the people of Israel. All three are bound up in one another. The point is that the future of the people of Israel is intimately related to the future of this promised descendant of David who will bring blessing for the people. What is striking is that many of these promises are seen to be further fulfilments of the promises made to Abraham in Genesis 12. It may be worth looking up those verses at the end of the study for a comparison. There is much in 2 Samuel 7 v 8-16 to thrill us. It would take weeks to go through all the subsequent links and references in the Bible that centre on this passage. You will need to be very selective and focus only on a few, to avoid straying too much from the text.

7. What does God promise about David's descendant (v 12-16)? There are several promises here. Some would be fulfilled by David's immediate descendants, but ultimately they are fulfilled in Christ.
- The descendant will build a house for God (v 12-13)
- The descendant will be God's son forever (v 14-15)
- The descendant will rule forever (v 16)

8. What does God promise to His people (v 10)? A place to be their home, where there is no evil, suffering or fighting.

EXPLORE MORE
Note: Although explore more is generally an optional part of the Bible study, in this case the questions are essential to understanding 2 Samuel 7 correctly, and need to be answered before tackling question 9 below.
Look again at the promises made to David, particularly those about his descendant and God's people. How would they be fulfilled?
David's descendant. **What is the temple that would be built? (See 1 Kings 8 v 17-19 and John 2 v 19-21.)** Solomon, David's son who would succeed him, would be the one to build David's "house for God" (ie: the temple). But this was only a partial fulfilment. Since the temple represented God's presence with His people, then the ultimate fulfilment must be Jesus as Immanuel—"God with us" (Matthew 1 v 23; John 2 v 19-21). He has provided forgiveness so that sinful people can live with a holy God!
Who would be the son (v 14) whose kingdom would last forever (v 13)? (See Mark 1 v 11 and Revelation 5 v 13.) The kings descended from David were wonderfully privileged—they were known as the sons of God (eg: Psalm 2);

and yet, we only have to look at the sinful failures and rebellion against God of the subsequent kings of Israel (beginning with David's own son, Solomon!) to realise that this promise would not be properly fulfilled in David's immediate descendants. Similarly, the kingdom of Israel first divided under the reign of Solomon's son, and then was taken over by various superpowers. The political kingdom of Israel could not fulfil the prophecy of a throne established forever (v 16). Only Jesus would fit this role perfectly. Jesus is the Son (Mark 1 v 11; Hebrews 1 v 5). He is the one (the Root and Offspring of David—Revelation 22 v 16) pictured in Revelation 5 v 13, whose kingdom will last forever.

How and why would the son be punished (v 14)? (See 2 Corinthians 5 v 21 and Galatians 3 v 13.) Despite the sin of the Israelite kings, God's covenant would not be revoked. God would have to punish them, but His love would never leave the line. The ultimate fulfilment though would be that Jesus would receive the "rod", though not for His own sin (see 2 Corinthians 5 v 21 and Galatians 3 v 13).

How and why would God's everlasting love (v 15) be shown to the son? (See John 10 v 17 and Romans 1 v 4.) God's love for Jesus didn't end when Jesus died on the cross (as some people believed, seeing this death only as the curse of God); in fact, John 10 v 17 makes it clear that Jesus' willingness to lay down His life in this way was precisely the reason why God loved Him. That God's love for Jesus continued is shown by the fact that three days later He raised Jesus from death (Romans 1 v 4), proving that Jesus is the eternally loved Son of God.

God's people. **How would v 10-11a be fulfilled? (See Revelation 21 v 1-4 and 22-27.)** The land of Israel never achieved this

ideal. Ultimately it is heaven!

Note: Like the promises of God to Abraham in Genesis 12, 2 Samuel 7 is one of those key passages pivotal to our understanding of the whole Bible. Help your group to grasp the cast-iron certainty of these promises, and their major importance in the subsequent history of Israel. Notice that:

• death cannot annul the promise (v 12-13)
• sin cannot destroy the promise (v 14-15)
• time will not exhaust the promise (v 16).

It is striking that throughout Israel's darkest days, these prophecies about David's family line would be constantly reiterated by the prophets. They stuck for dear life to the hope that one day God's promised "Messiah" ("Anointed One") would come (eg: Isaiah 11 v 1). So, when Matthew writes his genealogy of Jesus Christ (see Matthew 1), he must have been bristling with excitement!

9. APPLY: Today Christians look forward to the promised return of Jesus Christ in power and glory. What confidence in God do the fulfilled promises of 2 Samuel 7 give us? We are in a similar position to the people of Israel living after the time of David. We are waiting for the fulfilment of the promise that Jesus Christ will return again. But we also have the privilege of looking back in history and seeing how God's promises to David have already been fulfilled in Jesus Christ (see Explore More section above). When we see that God's promises to David were fulfilled, even after a thousand years, we can have confidence that the promises of Jesus' return will also be fulfilled.

Stress the importance of knowing and remembering the history of what God has already done, as recorded in the Bible, so that we will be able confidently to trust in God for the future.

- **What new things can we see about Jesus and His work for us, as we learn about God's promises to David and the history of their fulfilment?** Allow people to share discoveries that they have made in the course of this session. These will vary according to how much of the Bible group members already know.

- **How should confidence in Christ's return affect the way we live now?** Answers will probably be similar to those discussed in Session Two Q10. In the light of Christ's return, the New Testament teaches Christians to… say "No" to ungodliness and worldly passions (Titus 2 v 12-13); encourage one another by meeting together (Hebrews 10 v 25); be patient, stand firm and don't grumble (James 5 v 7-8); be prepared, self-controlled and set their hopes on the life to come (1 Peter 1 v 13); pray, love one another deeply and use the gifts given by God to serve others to the praise of God (1 Peter 4 v 7-11) etc.

10. What does David praise God for (v 18-24)? Notice David's humility and God's grace in v 18-19. Why does David's line

deserve such blessing? They don't! It is only because of God's grace! David praises God for His sovereign will in v 20-21. He praises God's uniqueness in v 22-24 and the works He has done among His people, Israel.

11. What does David pray for (v 25-29)? He asks God to do what He has already promised. Thus David is praying in line with God's character, God's will and God's agenda.

12. APPLY: Is our praise and adoration marked by similar things? If not, why not? If we prayed like David, what would have to change about the content of our prayers? Do we share David's joy? "Dead is the soul that has ceased to be amazed at the love of God!" Discuss how this session can help us to see why we might not share David's joy (eg: we don't know God's promises; we have forgotten how God has always fulfilled His promises in the past etc).
Often we pray in line with our character, will and agenda, not God's. Discuss how our prayers sound different to David's.

2 Samuel 11 – 12
AN ABJECT SINNER

THE BIG IDEA
Sin is always seen and judged by God, but can also be forgiven by Him.

SUMMARY
Up to this point in the story, David has seemed to be very impressive. He has had wonderful promises from God, he has

brought the ark to Jerusalem, and, by the end of 2 Samuel 10, many of David's enemies have been conquered and subjugated. But this chapter shows how flawed David really is.

It is a mistake to think that David is near perfect and that this episode is out of character. Certainly he loves the Lord and is godly. And yet here we see the man as he really is—a weak sinner.

The books of Samuel themselves have pointed to David's character flaws—David has practiced deception before in 1 Samuel 21, the result being the death of 85 priests (1 Samuel 22 v 18-19). Later, in 1 Samuel 25, David's hot temper nearly results in a massacre of innocent people, but for the intervention of a wise and godly woman. What is amazing about 2 Samuel 11–12 is not that David sins, but that God, in His wisdom and sovereignty, uses this weak king for His eternal salvation purposes, and also that God can forgive frail sinners such as David and us.

These chapters should not surprise us. They stand as lessons, first, in the dire consequences of sin, and second, the wonderful grace of God. This session will focus largely on the first lesson, and the next session on Psalm 51 will focus largely on the second.

Note: Obviously these are long passages to read. It may be best to encourage people to read the chapters beforehand, and then re-read only the central section, 12 v 1-14, during the Bible study. Also, because of the length of the story and the number of questions in the Bible study, there is no explore more in this session.

GUIDANCE ON QUESTIONS

1. Have you ever been "knocked off balance" by the sinfulness of a fellow-Christian? Do you ever surprise yourself by how sinful you can be? Without letting out confidential information or mentioning details that can reveal identities, discuss why you were so unprepared for what happened. You will need to exercise careful discretion in tackling this question. In some cases, depending on the particular situation in your church or the people involved in your group, you may prefer to leave it out altogether. Or people could think about it at home and then simply discuss their conclusions. Where discussion takes place during the Bible study, it is important not to let things degenerate into a gossip or grumbling session. The key point—and it's an important one—is that most of us tend to underestimate the extent or depth of sin, in our own hearts and in others. Again, we judge by appearances, constantly forgetting that "the heart is deceitful above all things" (Jeremiah 17 v 9).

2. What is the train of events that led to David's sin? At what points could he have stopped? The progress of verses 2-4 echo the original sin of Eve in the Garden of Eden. She saw, she took, she tasted—David saw, he took, he tasted. There is a horrible familiarity about it! David could easily have stopped if he had wanted to. He could have averted his gaze, he could have not inquired about her, he could have not ordered the messengers to get her, he could have resisted sleeping with her. He did none of these. While it is true that God doesn't let us be tempted beyond what we can bear (1 Corinthians 10 v 13), often we refuse to go out the exit when God provides it! It is often said that, by looking at verse 1, David should not have been hanging around the palace, but should have been at war. Had he been so, then he would not have committed this sin. There is certainly some truth in this, though bearing in mind David's past history, it seems all he needed was an opportunity and a motive and he could do anything. Such is the evil in the human heart. Certainly though, there is a lesson to learn here about not placing oneself in tempting situations. The devil puts idle hands to work! What may also be true is that David had grown complacent, and instead of leading his nation out to battle, he let others do his work for him.

Notice that Bathsheba is simply called "the woman" by the narrator. Nor do we ever find out about her feelings. It's as if to highlight the baseness of David's lust. Love has no place here—he "takes" another's wife; it is simply lust. Notice the reference to Bathsheba's purity (v 4), contrasting with David's impurity.

3. APPLY: What do these verses teach us about temptation? Can we learn anything about resisting temptation?

Temptation comes to us more easily in some situations than in others. But temptation is not the same as actual sin, and it doesn't inevitably lead to sin. In order for temptation to become sin we must give in to it, but temptation can be resisted. The question is: what will we choose to do when we are tempted?

Wise Christians will take steps to avoid situations in which they are more easily tempted.

Why not get your group to share some examples or ideas about how this can be done? Look again at 1 Corinthians 10 v 13 (see notes for Q2 above) and reflect on how this can help us when we are tempted.

4. How did David try and cover up his sin?

One of the horrible lessons we learn from this story is how one sin inevitably leads to another. Here lust leads to adultery, which leads to deception, which leads to murder!

5. How does David's behaviour compare to that of Uriah in this chapter?

The immediate consequences of David's sin are that Bathsheba becomes pregnant, and thus at risk of scandal and shame, since her husband, Uriah the Hittite, is away from home, fighting with the Israelite army. The immediate consequence for David is that he is also in danger of being exposed to scandal and shame, so he has to act deceptively, and ultimately, murderously, to cover up what he has done.

A striking parallel forms in this passage between David and Uriah. Uriah is a Hittite (ie: a foreigner). Here the foreign soldier behaves with more integrity and honour than God's Israelite covenant king. David's scheme is to get Uriah home from war and to sleep with Bathsheba to cover up the pregnancy and thus the sin. The plan fails. Verse 11 is pivotal. Uriah won't have his pleasure while his God (represented by the ark) and his fellow soldiers are fighting, as opposed to David who is happy to have his pleasure while everyone else is fighting. Even when drunk, Uriah won't comply (v 13). Sadly, Uriah is too honourable for his own, or rather David's, good! Thus, David's plot is hatched to have Uriah killed in battle at the front line. Notice how David is also willing to risk Joab's reputation as commander, and also shed other innocent lives (v 24), simply to cover his sin. But apparently it works—the immediate consequences seem to have been sorted to David's satisfaction!

6. By the end of the chapter all looks well. But what does the writer remind us of in verse 27? Why is this so significant?

David's sin may have been covered up to human eyes, but not to God's: "The thing David had done displeased the Lord" (v 27). It is God's verdict that matters. He is the one who can see into human hearts. God has been conspicuous by His absence in this chapter—the focus has been on David. But we cannot hide our sin from Him. Ironically, David had said to Joab in verse 25 (literally): "May this thing not be displeasing in your eyes!" It is displeasing in God's eyes though. Verse 27, and the next verse, form the hinge on which the whole passage turns. David's life would never be the same again.

7. How does Nathan's story get David to see his sin? What does this reveal about sinful human hearts? Nathan's story is deliberately designed to reveal David's sin. Nathan recounts the story of a sin apparently committed by one of David's subjects. This works because of the common tendency of sinful human hearts to quickly and easily spot sin in others, while remaining blind to our own sinfulness. (Compare Matthew 7 v 1-5.) So David quickly recognises the sin committed by the rich character of Nathan's story for what it truly is—a matter of injustice provoking anger and outrage, and even deserving death! But it takes Nathan's chilling words: "You are the man!" (v 7) for David also to recognise that he is guilty of the same abhorrent sin. At that moment, David understands that God sees everything.

8. What does Nathan say the real problem is? Verses 7-10 show the real cause of David's sin. He had despised the "word of the Lord" (v 9), and God Himself (v 10). After all God had done for him, still David wanted more for himself!

9. What is God's judgment on David's sin? The sword would never depart from David's house (v 10). The subsequent chapters outline the tragic consequences of his sin. A rape committed by one of his sons leads to murder, which leads to anarchy. Three sons are killed, and the line never fully recovers. It shows more clearly than ever how sin reaps its own rewards. Verses 11-12 would literally come true (see 2 Samuel 16 v 21-22).

10. How does God show grace towards David in this passage? Verse 1 is actually the first sign of God's grace. He sends a prophet to David. God could have let David go and never forgiven him. But the first step on the way back is for the sin to be recognised. God's word, even in judgment, is actually a sign of grace!

11. What is David's reaction to God's word? (Compare David's response in verse 13 with that of Saul in 1 Samuel 13 v 11-15 and 15 v 19-26.) Verse 13 reveals the key difference between David and Saul. David repented sincerely. When confronted by the word of the Lord he did not shirk its demand. Whereas Saul, in 1 Samuel 13, tries to justify himself and then again in 1 Samuel 15, having just committed the same sin of ignoring God's instructions. This is what shows us that Saul's "repentance" in 1 Samuel 15 v 24-25 is fake.

12. APPLY: What do these verses teach us about God's judgment? What do they teach us about the importance of listening to the "word of the Lord"? God's grace is seen, not just in His forgiveness, but in His judgment. Who knows where David would have ended up, or where we would be, if God never stepped in!

David's downfall came about because he "despised the word of the Lord" about sexual sin. This story underlines the crucial importance of always taking God's word seriously. And Saul's rejection by God (1 Samuel 15 v 26-29), after he had failed to obey God's word yet again, demonstrates clearly that we will not be given endless opportunities to "try again". (See Hebrews 3 v 7-13.)

13. How can God forgive this sin? What should happen to David, according to Leviticus 20 v 10 and 24 v 17? Compare Romans 3 v 23-26. Verse 13b is surely one of the most extraordinary statements in the Old Testament. How can God forgive such sin? If we bristle at the apparent injustice, then we don't have to look far into our hearts to see where we also stand! David deserved death (Leviticus 20 v 10 and 24 v 17), but instead, he was forgiven. God's grace is astounding. Such forgiveness can only be seen to be just through the cross of Christ (Romans 3 v 25), where God, in the very act that will make forgiveness of sinners possible, is shown to be just as He punishes all sin in Jesus Christ. However, God's forgiveness comes at a great price—the accursed death of His own Son.

14. What do the loss of David's illegitimate child, and the birth of Solomon, tell us about how God deals with sin? While David is forgiven, he must still live with the tragic consequences of his sin. This is seen in the death of his baby (v 14). David's pleading with God shows that he knows God to be gracious, yet this time, God's verdict must stand. However, this story does end in grace. The birth of Solomon is seen to be a mark of God's love. It is striking that from this son will come the temple and also eventually the Messiah. What is even more incredible is that out of this line God will bring the Saviour, who will deal with all sin. Out of this terrible evil, God works His ultimate good.

15. APPLY: Looking back over the whole story, what have you learned about...
- **human hearts and sin's consequences?** If we despise God's word our hearts become hardened, and it's easy to commit more and worse sins. And our minds become foolish, thinking we can cover up what we've done, even from God.

- **God's judgment:** It is inevitable. In spite of what we imagine, God does see everything we do and He will judge all sin.

- **God's forgiveness?** God has gone to incredible lengths and cost to make forgiveness possible, while also treating all sin with complete justice. God can only do this through the cross of Jesus Christ. We can only be forgiven because of the cross of Jesus Christ.

---

5 Psalm 51

AN UNDESERVED FORGIVENESS

THE BIG IDEA
Christians can be confident that God justly forgives sin.

SUMMARY
As the heading to Psalm 51 suggests, it was written in the aftermath of 2 Samuel 11–12. Last session we saw how David was plunged into the depths of sin as an adulterer, liar, murderer and cheat. But the word of God came to him in the form of Nathan and so his restoration began. If the story in 2 Samuel 11–12 tells us the details of the sin, then this passage teaches us what was going on in David's heart. And yet, it also speaks to each one of us who wrestles with

sin, and shows us the wonderful depths of God's love in forgiving the sinner. We also learn what is involved for our part—heartfelt repentance.

Psalm 51 seems at first to be repetitive, though there is a definite progression. David moves from humble confession through to forgiveness and renewal, and then his own response in longing to tell others and declare God's praises. It functions more like an upward spiral, coming back to the same themes but from a different angle. Once again, we'll find ourselves being led to Christ, the Anointed One par excellence.

GUIDANCE ON QUESTIONS

1. How often do we hear the word "forgiveness" in our society? What words are more likely to be used when someone has been wronged? Perhaps your group could discuss high-profile cases of crime or injustice. What were the reactions of the victims? If forgiveness was mentioned, were any reasons for that forgiveness also mentioned? Mostly, it is Christians who are willing to forgive in these traumatic situations, because they know what it is to have been forgiven by God.

2. On what grounds does David appeal to God for forgiveness (v 1-2)? David's first words are for mercy. He recognises his sin, but the ground of mercy is the grace of God, God's unfailing love and great compassion. The word in verse 1 for "unfailing love" is "hesed", the covenant love of God to His people. It is on this ground that David appeals to God. He knows that God's love is all consuming and fully committed. This is what God is like! (Compare Exodus 34 v 5-7; Jonah 4 v 2.) David appeals to God's character, which has been revealed through His word. In this way,

God is bound by His promises. Notice the effect on David of truly understanding God's character. In verse 2 David fully believes that God is gracious enough to wash away all iniquities and blot out his sins (To appreciate how astonishing David's confidence is, see notes on Q7 below).

3. What has David discovered about himself (v 3-5)? These verses show that David, unlike Saul in 1 Sam 13 and 15, is truly repentant.

• Notice how many times the word "my" or "mine" or "I" comes up—David is in no doubt that he is the guilty party.

• His sin is always before him (v 3)—ie: his conscience is racked.

• He uses three words for sin (v 2-3): transgression, iniquity, and sin. All three mean a deliberate choice to rebel.

• David knows his sin is ultimately against God and against Him alone (Compare 2 Samuel 11 v 27b). God is the one offended—despite the horrific consequences for the people involved— therefore God is entirely just in punishing David's sin.

• David knows his sin is from birth. In fact, he has been enmeshed in sin even from before the day he was born. He's a natural born rebel!

4. How do you think he has come to this discovery (see 2 Samuel 12, especially v 9a and the beginning of v 11)? Through God's word—both the Law of Moses and the words of Nathan the prophet. Nathan has already told David that he had despised the word of the Lord when he sinned with Bathsheba (see 2 Samuel 12 v 9), so clearly, David knew God's word. He would have had the Law of Moses (the first five books of the Old Testament), which records the relationship between God and the people He had chosen—the nation of Israel—through the history of Israel up to, and beyond, the exodus from Egypt, and through the rules and regulations that God had given to Moses to govern every aspect of life in Israel.

God's promises and pronouncements to His people through the ages had been written down in black and white. Anything that God subsequently did with Israel could be measured against His words. The history of Israel shows God to be utterly faithful to His character and His promises. The people of Israel, by contrast, are shown to be ungrateful, fickle and rebellious and not a single character from the Old Testament is untouched by sin.

What David can discover from the Scriptures has also been borne out in his own experience. Despite David's past failings, God has always remained faithful, yet in this latest incident, David has chosen again to rebel against God.

5. APPLY: Why is it important that we understand God's character as revealed in His word? If we don't, we won't be able to have the confidence in God's mercy and the assurance of His forgiveness that David was able to have, even after he had committed such terrible sins. We need to remember that, since the Garden of Eden, the devil's greatest tactic has been to lead us to doubt God's word. So the devil persuades people that the Bible is unclear ("it depends on your interpretation"), that it is untrue ("the Bible has been disproved"), and that it is unfair ("God restricts our freedom and keeps us in slavery"). Yet the history of Israel shows us that God speaks clearly, His character—not just His words—is truth, and He is utterly fair, to His enormous cost when it comes to the question of forgiveness for sins (see Q7 below).

• **How will this help us in the Christian life?** Christians who truly understand God's grace are able to come to Him and freely confess all sins—the first step to restoration. But those who only think of God as an angry judge will try to hide or deny their sin, with disastrous consequences for their fellowship with God, their ability to help others in the Christian life and their own joy (compare Psalm 51 v 8). See 1 John 1 v 8-10.

• **What happens when we have a poor understanding of our own sin?** A weak view of sin leads to a weak view of grace! Do we acknowledge our depravity, like David? Do we think sin is serious? Or are we tame with sin?

6. How is David's confidence seen in these verses? Notice how David's confidence is in God's help—"you teach me wisdom in the inmost place" (v 6)—and asking God to cleanse him (v 7). God alone can do these things. David sees what God's standards are—"truth in the inner parts" ie: the heart (v 6). How can we keep God's law in our hearts? The answer is that God must create a pure heart in us (v 10). Thus, only God can cleanse us and make us whiter than snow (compare Isaiah 1 v 18). Hyssop was prescribed by the law (Leviticus 14 v 1-7) for the cleansing of infectious skins diseases like leprosy, which is a good picture of sin! Notice verse 8—David will rejoice once again. Crushed people can rejoice again! But only through God's restoration.

EXPLORE MORE
Do you think the Christian's confidence should be greater or lesser than David's? Why do you think that? See Colossians 1 v 25-26. Christians have received "the word of God in its fulness"—what was in previous

ages and generations a mystery that had been kept hidden has now been disclosed to us. Because of the word of the Lord, David knew that only God could teach him wisdom and cleanse him from his sin. He also knew that God would do these things. But we can see how God does these things, and how He has kept His promises to do them—in Jesus Christ. So Christians should have even greater confidence than David in God's ability and willingness to forgive and change us, but only if we respond in total faith to God's word, as David did. The question for us is: do we trust "the word of God in its fulness", that we have received?

How have Christians been taught "wisdom in the inmost place" by God? See 1 John 2 v 20-27 (especially v 20 and 27). What is that wisdom? See Colossians 2 v 3 and 2 Timothy 3 v 15.
1 John 2 v 20-27: Christians have been anointed "from the Holy One" ie: the Holy Spirit, enabling them to know the truth (v 20). John told his Christian readers that they did not need anyone else to teach them (v 27), meaning that they did not need to listen to those who would come with a message other than the one that John's readers had "heard from the beginning" ie: the apostles' teaching (v 24).
Colossians 2 v 3: In the New Testament, wisdom is found in Jesus Christ.
2 Timothy 3 v 15: We become wise by turning to Him for salvation. So God teaches people "wisdom in the inmost place" by giving them the Holy Spirit, who convinces them of the apostles' teaching—that they need to turn to Jesus Christ to be saved from their sins.
How have Christians been "cleansed" and "washed" by God? See John 15 v 3, Ephesians 5 v 25-26 and Titus 3 v 4-5.
John 15 v 3; Ephesians 5 v 25-26: Both of these passages refer to the fact that

Christians are cleansed by the word of Christ.
Titus 3 v 4-5: Christians are "washed" when they are born again by the Holy Spirit.
So what do people need to become acceptable (clean) to God and to be truly wise? What does this mean for Christian outreach and evangelism?
People need to become Christians, by the power of God's word—the message about Jesus Christ—and the Holy Spirit. This means that Christian outreach and evangelism must centre on both proclaiming God's word and praying for the work of the Holy Spirit.

7. What are the various longings that David expresses in these verses?
- **v 9—a new purity:** Notice how David wants God to hide His face from David's sins—but not from David himself—and to blot out his transgressions. A moment's thought reveals just what an extraordinary request this is. How can God completely blot out our sins so that He cannot see them? How can He justly do this? Only through the cross, where sin was punished, but in Jesus, not the sinner (see Romans 3 v 25-26). David didn't see the cross. But he did see in God's character the certainty that He would do something about sin. So God looks on us and sees "blameless" people! Have we understood how remarkable it is that God does "remember our sins no more" (Hebrews 8 v 12, quoting Jeremiah 31 v 34)?

- **v 10—a new power:** If David is not to repeat the failure that resulted in him needing forgiveness and purification by God, he must have a "new spirit" that will steadfastly do what God wants. In the New Testament we have the reassurance of God's Spirit at work in us. God doesn't just forgive—He transforms!

- **v 11—a new presence:** David longs that God wouldn't take His Spirit from him. He probably has in mind here Saul (see 1 Samuel 16 v 14). In His grace, God restored David to kingship, though he did have to live with the consequences of his sin. God never leaves His people on the shelf. Forgiven sinners are always welcome again in God's work and family.

- **v 12—a new pleasure:** David longs to have the depth of relationship that he had with God before. He longs to have back that enthusiastic heart. It's one of the dangers of being a Christian for many years—we can lose our first joy and enthusiasm. But praise God!—the Christian life has many new beginnings and restorations!

8. Looking at verse 13, what is David's aim now he has been forgiven? All of David's longings lead up to v 13—David will teach others from his own experience of God's grace, so that others will turn back to God! This psalm is evidence of that!

9. What other longings and intentions make up David's response to God in these verses?

- **v 14-15:** *A longing to praise God:* Notice that it is God's righteousness that David praises! And in particular, His ability to declare unrighteous people righteous without being unrighteous Himself! (See question 7 above.)

- **v 16-17:** *A longing to please God:* These verses do not tell us that God really thought the sacrificial system was a mistake. Rather, what David understood was that the heart of the person making the sacrifice was important too. Religion without heart is cold and meaningless! (Compare 1 Samuel 15 v 22). All the Old

Testament prophets saw this—there are plenty of examples to choose from!

- **v 18-19:** *A longing to be prospered by God, for His glory:* David asked that God's people would be blessed. He realised that his own spiritual health affected the health of the nation. And similarly, just as he was able to rejoice in God's goodness and blessing, so he wanted his people to share in the same joy. And all of this so that others would also respond to God in praise and thanksgiving. We are part of God's people. Just as our own spiritual health is our concern, so should the whole body's spiritual health also be our concern.

10. What is it that God requires of us in verses 16-17? "A broken and contrite heart" (v 17) ie: a humble and repentant sinner—not someone who is proud and self-righteous.

11. APPLY: How will we act, as individual Christians and as churches, if we share these longings that David has spoken about in Psalm 51? Go through David's longings again. Discuss those that have particularly struck people in your group, and those that you feel are lacking among yourselves and in your church. What practical differences can be seen when people long for these things?

- **How does David's attitude in verse 13 challenge us?** Because of our salvation, and the joy it has brought us, it should be our desire to teach transgressors God's ways and help sinners turn back to Him. Because of our own experiences of God's goodness, we can invite people to "taste and see that the Lord is good" (Psalm 34 v 8). If that's not happening in your church or among the people in your group, you could take the opportunity to discuss why.

6 2 Samuel 22
AN AWESOME GOD

THE BIG IDEA
It is God who gives His anointed one the victory—ultimately, Jesus Christ and His victory over sin, death and the devil by the cross.

SUMMARY
This final session brings us to the end of 1 and 2 Samuel, but to the heart of David. This psalm (it appears also as Psalm 18) ends the books, while Hannah's prayer (1 Sam 2) started them. The same themes occur in both: God's greatness, faithfulness and the fact there is no one like God. We are meant to see that behind all the events that have been played out on the human stage, the hand of God has been at work, sometimes clearly, sometimes behind the scenes.

In 2 Samuel 22 David looks back over events involving Saul and all his other enemies (see v 1), and remembers how God has watched over him. David shows his deep understanding of the God he serves, and, with the benefit of hindsight, he can now see that God's hand has been at work, and so He praises Him. David's hindsight of the past helps him to live with foresight in the present. David's only concern is to glorify God. As Christians, we can appreciate much of what David says as we also know it to be true through Jesus. The challenge is whether the God we claim to know is the same as David's, or whether, in comparison, our view of God is shallow. David truly knew God!

The psalm finishes on a tremendous note of praise. The final verses (v 47-51) sum up the whole psalm and, once again, find their fulfilment in "great David's greater Son".

Verse 51 echoes something that Hannah had prayed back in 1 Sam 2 v 10—surely God will exalt His Anointed One (see Philippians 2 v 9-11). God's unfailing kindness ("hesed"—His covenant love, the love and faithfulness that God displays when He makes His covenant with His people) is seen in His commitment to His king and His people. So at the end of history we'll be with the King in heaven, praising His name, and we'll see God's promises to David (2 Sam 7) in all their glorious technicolour!

GUIDANCE ON QUESTIONS
1. Share some commonly-held views about what God is like. Where do these views come from? If you, as a Christian, had the opportunity to talk to someone with one of these views about what God is like, what points would you try to get across? It should quickly become apparent that popular views of God are very different from the God of the Bible. People are not able to come to an accurate understanding of God through their own ideas. Humans always end up "creating" God in their own image—eg: see Isaiah 44 v 10-13 and Romans 1 v 22-23. Instead, we need to listen to what God has already revealed about Himself in His word.

2. In verses 2-4, how many different images does David use to describe God? How does each image help us to understand God better? v 2—rock, fortress, deliverer; v 3—"shield and horn of my salvation", stronghold, refuge, saviour; v 4—"worthy of praise".
Go through each description and discuss

what it tells us about God eg: rock—a firm place to build on, not unstable or likely to get swept away by weather or disaster; fortress—a well-protected place of safety that you can hide inside etc. In these verses it's as if David is replaying every period of stress he went through with Saul (see 1 Sam 18–31). Notice how many words of "salvation" there are here. David didn't "see" God working like this at the time—and yet now we can see that God's hand was very clearly at work in protecting David.

3. What was David's first port of call in his time of distress? These verses are no exaggeration—death must have felt very close in those grim days when Saul was hunting him down. David's feelings in such situations are graphically recorded in many of the psalms (eg: Psalm 22 v 1, 6, 12-15 etc.). David's first action was to call to the Lord (v 7). There's no point having a refuge if we don't turn to Him! Note David's utter helplessness (v 5). Yet even death is in God's hands! V 7 shows both our need to pray and also the amazing grace of God in answering. If David could pray, how much more can we (see Hebrews 4 v 14-16)!

4. What do verses 8-20 show us about David's understanding of God? Are there any hints from these verses as to where David's understanding of God came from? (Compare Exodus 19 v 18.) From v 8-16 we can see David understood God to be awesome, terrifying in His power, sovereign over His creation and angry against the enemies of His anointed one. From v 18-20 we can see David was confident of God's love for and even delight in him (v 20). This passage is full of picture language—these things didn't happen literally— but David knew God was at work behind the scenes.

David's understanding of God comes from various episodes played out in Israel's history: verses 7-8 remind us of Sinai (see Exodus 19 v 18); verses 9-12 have echoes of some of the judgment of God upon Egypt during the exodus. What is remarkable is that the God who is magnificently awesome in this way is the same God who works in David's life to protect and rescue him.

5. In verses 17-20, David records three ways in which God has saved him. What are they? David's salvation is seen in rescue (v 17-18), support (v 19), and freedom (v 20). Thus the joy that David expresses in verses 2-4 is seen to be authentic from his experience of God in times of bitter trouble.

6. APPLY: What things can prevent us from praying as David did (v 7), when we are in difficulty? There are two fundamental misconceptions that people have about God, both of which will prevent us from praying to Him in times of trouble.
1. Believing God is not able to help us.
2. Believing God is not willing to help us.
People may not actually say this, but often it is what they believe deep down, shown by the fact they don't immediately call to the Lord in their distress. The question we must ask is whether David's God is the same God we know and love. How big is our God?

• **How will praying help us in these situations?** When we pray, we are confronted with the question of who it is that we are speaking to, why we can or can't expect Him to listen to us, and whether we are willing to trust and obey Him. It brings us back to the basics of our Christian faith. When we pray, God hears us (v 7b)—He may or may not take us out of the situation, but He will give us "grace to help us in our time of need" (Hebrews

4 v 16). Later, when we look back at what has happened, we can be confident that it was God that brought us through a difficult time, and our understanding of what God is truly like is deepened.

- **How would an understanding of God, like David's, help us to live as Christians?** When we understand God as David does—supremely powerful and yet devoted to His people—we have confidence to pray to Him and trust Him for the outcomes of difficult situations.

- **How can we help ourselves to develop this kind of understanding and experience of God?** David had learned what God is like from the history of Israel, and so can we! David had also learned from his own past experiences and so can we! Get people to discuss how we can help each other do this.

7. What do these verses (2 Samuel 22 v 21-31) tell us about David's desires and heart? David knew he was a sinner (see Psalm 51), yet longed to be blameless in following God. John Calvin said: "David … sometimes fell into sin through the weakness of the flesh, but he never desisted in following after godliness, nor deserted in the service to which God had called him."

EXPLORE MORE
What is David not saying in these verses? (Compare Psalm 51. See also Romans 3 v 10-12.)
So what is he saying? (See Proverbs 3 v 5-6 and Matthew 5 v 1-12).
How have verses 21-25 been fulfilled literally? (See 1 Peter 2 v 22.)
How can these verses be true of Christians? (See 2 Corinthians 5 v 21.)
At first sight 2 Samuel 22 v 21-31 seems a little disturbing. Surely David isn't saying

that his life has been good enough for God (justification by works)? Clearly not, when you compare Psalm 51, where David confesses both his sinful actions (v 4) and his sinful nature (v 5) to God. Romans 3 v 10-12 agrees by stating that no one is righteous or without sin. Instead, David seems to be saying what the whole Bible says—that the Christian, the person who is made righteous because of their faith, will seek to live by God's laws and with God's help is able to do it. David is not claiming sinless perfection; rather, that he has sought to live God's way. For such a person there is great blessing (see Proverbs 3 v 5-6). It is this sort of attitude that Jesus demands of the Christian in the beatitudes (Matthew 5 v 1-12). Of course, in Jesus these verses would be literally fulfilled (1 Peter 2 v 22)! And Christians can have His righteousness (2 Corinthians 5 v 21)!

8. How is David able to win victory over his enemies? Notice how many times David says "God", or "He" and "You" in reference to God, when he explains why he is able to defeat his enemies. His hope is clearly in God to defeat his enemies. It is God who gives His anointed one the victory eg: v 33—"it is God who arms me with strength"; v 34—"he enables me to stand on the heights"; v 35—"He trains my hands for battle"; v 36—"you give me your shield of victory" and "you stoop down to make me great"; v 40—"You armed me with strength for battle" and "you made my adversaries bow at my feet"; v 41—"You made my enemies turn their backs in flight"; v 44—"you have delivered me" and "you have preserved me"; v 48—"the God who avenges me," and "who puts the nations under me"; v 49—"who sets me free from my enemies", "you exalted me above my foes" and "you rescued me"; v 51—"he gives his king great victories".

9. How are David's victories over his enemies described? What impression does this give? v 38—crushed, destroyed; v 39—"they could not rise"; v 40—"my adversaries bow at my feet"; v 41—"my enemies turn their backs in flight"; v 42—"no one to save them"; v 43—"beat them as fine as the dust of the earth", "pounded and trampled them like mud in the streets"; v 45—"foreigners come cringing to me", "as soon as they hear me, they obey me"; v 46—"they all lose heart", "they come trembling from their strongholds".

The impression is one of utter defeat for David's enemies, and total victory for David.

EXPLORE MORE

How are these verses fulfilled in Jesus? Think about: • His victory (v 32-43): see Hebrews 2 v 14-15; Colossians 2 v 13-15. David defeated the enemies of Israel during his reign, but there would come a day when Israel was again threatened by surrounding nations (eg: 1 Kings 20 v 1). But Jesus has destroyed the devil for ever, and freed those who lived in slavery to the fear of death (Hebrews 2 v 14-15). Christ achieved His victory over the spiritual enemies of God on the cross (Col 2 v 13-15).

• **His rule over the nations (v 44-46): see Matthew 25 v 31-46; Revelation 19 v 11-16.** David had mixed success with the nations around him, but at the end of history Jesus Christ will be revealed as the supreme ruler of all the nations (Revelation 19 v 11-16). The nations will come to Him, for some, as their Lord and Saviour but for others, as their Judge (Matthew 25 v 31-46).

• **His final exaltation (v 47-52): see Philippians 2 v 9-11.** David became Israel's greatest king, but God has given Jesus the highest place (so that one day everyone will bow to Him) and the highest name (which one day everyone will confess) (Philippians 2 v 9-11).

10. APPLY: What qualities have you seen in the life of David, which, as a Christian, you would like to imitate in your own life?

• **From looking at the life of God's king, David, what have you learned about God's true King, Jesus? And how will that affect your life?** Spend time thinking over what people have learned from all the sessions. Encourage your group to share the things that have particularly struck or challenged them.